Helping Children See Jesus

ISBN: 978-1-933206-72-1

LAW AND GRACE
New Testament Volume 27
Galatians Part 2

Author: Marilyn P. Habecker
Illustrator: Frances H. Hertzler
Computer Graphic Artist: Ed Olson
Typesetting and Layout: Morgan Melton, Patricia Pope

© 2018 Bible Visuals International
PO Box 153, Akron, PA 17501-0153
Phone: (717) 859-1131
www.biblevisuals.org

All rights reserved. No part of this publication may be reproduced, stored in a retrieval system or transmitted in any form by any means, electronic, mechanical, photocopy, recording or otherwise, without the prior permission of the publisher, except as provided by USA copyright law.

RELATED ITEMS

To access related items (such as activities, memory verse posters and translated texts) please visit our web store at shop.biblevisuals.org and enter 1027 in the search box on the page.

FREE TEXT DOWNLOAD

To access a FREE printable copy of the teaching text (PDF format) in English or other available languages, enter S1027DL in the search box. Add the item to your cart, and use coupon code XTACSV17 at checkout. Once your order is processed you will receive an email with a link to the free download.

Christ hath redeemed us from the curse of the law, being made a curse for us. Galatians 3:13a

Lesson 1
WHAT IS THE LAW?

NOTE TO THE TEACHER

It is impossible to overemphasize the vital importance of the Epistle to the Galatians. We should always be thankful to God for this wonderful letter. If Paul had not corrected the Galatians, the truth of the Gospel of Christ might have been quenched in that province. Paul was used of God to preserve its purity.

In our study of the first two chapters of Galatians, we saw that the Galatians had begun to doubt the Apostle Paul's message of salvation by faith alone in Christ. They questioned the message partly because false teachers challenged Paul's apostleship. So Paul used one-third of his letter to prove that he really was an apostle. In chapters 3 and 4, Paul defends the Gospel. The first two chapters of the book are of a personal nature. Chapters 3 and 4 are doctrinal. In this volume, we will look deeply into the subjects of law and grace. Encourage your students to read these two chapters every day during the time you will be teaching these chapters.

When teaching the memory verse, explain that the expression "being made a curse for us" means that Christ died in our place.

Scripture to be studied: Galatians 3; Exodus 20:1–24:11; Leviticus 16

The *aim* of the lesson: To show that the Law was good, but it could not provide salvation.

What your students should *know*: That the Law served as a guide for Israel only until Christ came.

What your students should *feel*: Thankful that God does not expect them to keep the Law in order to belong to Him.

What your students should *do*:

Unsaved: Each one must turn wholly to Christ as Lord and Saviour.

Saved: Pray that this week they will be able to point an unsaved person to God's true way of salvation.

Lesson outline (For the teacher's and students' notebooks):

1. God gave the Law to Israel to show what sin is (Galatians 3:10, 19, 22).
2. In the Law God provided a system of sacrifices for the covering of sins.
3. The penalty for breaking the Law was death (Galatians 3:10).
4. The Law served as a guide until Christ came (Galatians 3:24-25).

The verse to be memorized:

Christ hath redeemed us from the curse of the law, being made a curse for us. (Galatians 3:13a)

THE LESSON

Do you know someone who thinks he must do something good in order to earn salvation? Then listen carefully.

Paul could scarcely believe what he'd heard. Was it possible that the Galatian Christians had been fooled so easily by men who did not preach the truth? Did they really believe that in addition to receiving Christ as Lord and Saviour they also had to follow the Law in order to be saved and remain saved?

"O foolish Galatians," Paul wrote to them, "you act as though someone had cast a spell on you so that you can't even think clearly!" Then he asked an important question: "Did you receive the Holy Spirit as a result of obeying the Law and doing its works? Or was it by hearing the message of the Gospel and believing it?"

What could the Galatians answer? When Paul had visited their cities, many Galatians had received Christ as their Saviour from sin. They knew that at that time the Holy Spirit had come to live in their hearts. Now false teachers persuaded them that they must earn their salvation by keeping the Law and observing ceremonies. So they became willing to depend on their own works rather than God's perfect gift. Imagine that!

"No man is justified by the Law in the sight of God," Paul said, "for the justified ones shall live by faith. And the Law is not of faith." Nothing could be clearer than this.

The Galatians still had some questions. Perhaps you have some of the same questions. What is this law which we're talking about? Why was it given? Since God knew that no one could ever keep the Law perfectly, why did He give it?

1. GOD GAVE THE LAW TO ISRAEL TO SHOW WHAT SIN IS
Galatians 3:10, 19, 22

Show Illustration #1

Let us imagine that you are going fishing. You arrive at a fine spot and cast your line into the water. While waiting for a bite, you notice a sign in large letters: NO FISHING. What are you doing? You are breaking the Law.

You are doing wrong by fishing in a place where fishing is not allowed. The sign tells you so. If there weren't any sign for you to read, you wouldn't know that fishing is not allowed. By reading the sign, you understand that you are doing wrong.

So it is with God's Law. God gave it to His people Israel so they would have a way of understanding right from wrong. If there were no law, a person might not know what sin is. The Law shows people they are sinners.

In the Law are instructions for worship, feasts, family life, getting along with neighbors, and many other things. The Law was strict and there was certain punishment for those who disobeyed it.

Some of the laws which God gave the Israelites concerned their thoughts and attitudes. God said, "You shall not covet." You are not to want to have for yourself something which already belongs to someone else. Was it possible for the Israelites to obey this law? Could the Galatians obey it? Can you obey it?

Suppose your friend has a new coat. (*Teacher:* Or name something that would be of interest to your class.) As soon as you see it, you think, Oh, I wish that coat were mine. That would be coveting. Even if you immediately realize that your thoughts are wrong, you are guilty of the sin of coveting.

– 18 –

2. IN THE LAW GOD PROVIDED A SYSTEM OF SACRIFICES FOR THE COVERING OF SINS
Leviticus 16

God's Law with its many commands is holy. It is just. It is good. (See Romans 7:12.) But it is rigid and unbending. To disobey a command is sin. (See Deuteronomy 27:26; Galatians 3:10.) And sin must be punished. But, because of His love, God provided with the Law a way for sinners to have their sins covered.

Show Illustration #2

He commanded each person who sinned, either knowingly or unknowingly, to bring an offering to the house of God. (See Exodus 29:10-25; Leviticus 4:1-35; 6:24-30.) Depending on the kind of sin, the offering was to be a bull, a goat, a ram, a lamb, or two turtledoves. (Turtledoves were to be brought by the very poor.) Each sacrifice had to be perfect.

3. THE PENALTY FOR BREAKING THE LAW WAS DEATH
Galatians 3:10

The sinner took his offering to the priest, who tied the animal to the brass altar. The offerer put his hand on the head of the animal and confessed his sin to God. He asked God to accept the animal in his place. The priest plunged a knife into the animal's throat. With his finger he put some blood on each corner of the altar and poured the rest beside the altar.

Parts of the animal were burned on the altar. The fire reminded the sinner of God's hatred of sin. Each sinner brought one offering, and then another, and yet another. Over and over again the animals died for the sins of the people. Once a year (on the holy Day of Atonement) the high priest made an offering to God for all the sins of the nation. That day a young bull was sacrificed. The high priest caught the blood in a basin and did what he alone was permitted to do (and do only once a year): he went into the most holy place.

Show Illustration #3

There the priest dipped his fingers into the basin of blood and sprinkled it on the lid of the ark, called the Mercy Seat. Seven times he sprinkled the blood on the ground. If the high priest did not do exactly as God had ordered, God would strike him dead. This would be his punishment for breaking God's holy law.

Each sinner who watched the animal sacrifices die realized how severe the penalty of the Law was. To disobey the Law by coveting, or lying, or stealing–or in any other way–meant death. That is why Paul told the Galatians, "Whoever tries to keep the demands of the Law is under a curse, for God's Word says, 'Cursed is every one who does not continue to do all things which are written in the book of the Law.'" (See Galatians 3:10; Deuteronomy 27:25.) The Law puts the curse of death on all who do not obey it perfectly.

4. THE LAW SERVED AS A GUIDE UNTIL CHRIST CAME
Galatians 3:24-25

Paul told the Galatians two reasons why God gave the Law. You will want to write these in your notebook.

GOD GAVE THE LAW BECAUSE:

1. He wanted His people to know how helpless and how sinful they were. (See Romans 3:20; Galatians 3:19.)
2. The Law was given to guide God's people until the coming of Christ. (See Galatians 3:19-25; Romans 10:4.) It was like a child's guide.

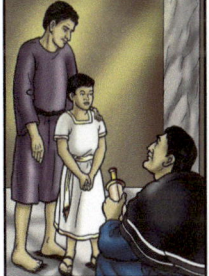
Show Illustration #4

In the days of Paul, both the Greeks and the Romans had servants who were called "child-guides." (In the English Bible the "child-guide" is called a "schoolmaster.") The "child-guide" was responsible to take his master's young boy to the school teacher. The child's guide was required to punish the child when he disobeyed him, and to teach him good habits. That is exactly what the Law did; it demanded punishment for those who did not obey it. It protected them by ordering sacrifices to cover their sins. It taught them to have good habits. But that was all the Law did for them. It never took away their sins. (See Hebrews 10:1, 4, 11.)

For 1,400 years the Law guided the Israelites. Then God sent His Son to earth. (See Galatians 4:4.) After His death everything was changed. The Lord Jesus and He alone had kept the Law perfectly. He never did anything wrong, He never said anything wrong, He never thought one wrong thing. When He died, He took upon Himself all the sins of every person who would ever live. (See Isaiah 53:5-6; 1 Peter 2:24; 3:18.) He died before you were born. But He died for every wrong thing that you have done or ever will do. He took the punishment for your sins so that you won't have to be punished for them eternally. Because of Him, we don't need the Law in order to be saved.

Perhaps you are one who has been trying to earn your salvation by doing good works or by obeying laws. Will you turn instead to the perfect One who gave His blood for you, the Lord Jesus Christ? Will you ask Him to forgive your sin? Do you believe He is the Son of God who died and rose again so that you can have eternal life? If you do, will you receive Him as your Saviour, your sin-bearer, right now?

If you are already a child of God, ask the Lord to lead you this week to someone who is trying to keep laws or do good works in order to earn salvation. Pray that you will be able to show that person God's true way of salvation.

Lesson 2
WHAT IS GRACE?

NOTE TO THE TEACHER

The Galatian Epistle was written by Paul to believers, rebuking them for their error in turning to law-keeping. Paul had presented the Gospel clearly when he was with the Galatians. But it became necessary to review and restate carefully the doctrine of salvation by grace through faith in Christ alone. Let this be an example to you, teacher: never assume that your students have fully understood a truth after one telling. Review it again and again. Build instruction upon instruction, remembering that review is a vital part of the learning process. (See Isaiah 28:10.)

In your review time, always allow your students to discuss the lesson, phrasing it in their own terms. A person has not really learned unless he/she can express his/her knowledge in his/her own words.

In the first lesson of this volume we discussed the Law. In this lesson we introduce grace. Grace is used almost constantly in contrast with law. Under law, God demands righteousness from man. Under grace, God gives righteousness to man. (See Romans 3:21-22; 8:3-4; Philippians 3:9.) Law is connected with Moses and works. Grace is related to Christ and faith. (John 1:17.) The Law promises blessing for those who are good. Grace offers salvation to those who are not good. Law demands that blessings be earned. Grace is God's free gift.

Scripture to be studied: Galatians 3 and 4; Genesis 37; 39:1–41:45; 45:1-16

The *aim* of the lesson: To show that God's grace is not merited. Because of His love for us and because of Christ's death for us, we receive His grace, His favor, kindness and mercy.

What your students should *know*: That grace is God's loving favor and kindness to all, even though no one deserves it.

What your students should *feel*: The wonder of God's grace.

What your students should *do*:
  Unsaved: Accept God's gracious gift of salvation right now.
  Saved: Remember to thank God each day for His grace.

Lesson outline (For the teacher's and students' notebooks):
1. Grace is the opposite of law (Galatians 1:6-7; 3:2-3, 5).
2. Grace is God's kindness, love and favor to those who do not deserve it.
3. Joseph's kindness to his brothers is an example of grace.
4. Because of God's grace, Christ died for all our sins (Galatians 3:13).

The verse to be memorized:

Christ hath redeemed us from the curse of the law, being made a curse for us. (Galatians 3:13a)

THE LESSON

You have probably sung about God's grace. Suppose you were asked to explain grace to someone who has never heard the word. Could you do it? Listen carefully.

1. GRACE IS THE OPPOSITE OF LAW
Galatians 1:6-7; 3:2-3, 5

The Law which God had given through Moses to His people, Israel, was stern. It was harsh. All of its commands (613 of them!) were to be obeyed. The person who disobeyed the Law was punished.

Show Illustration #5a

Once a man picked up sticks on the Sabbath Day (Saturday). God had said in the Law that the Sabbath Day was to be kept holy. It was a day to be used for resting and for worshiping Him. Gathering sticks was unlawful on the Sabbath; it was sin. So God told Moses, "The man shall be surely put to death: all the congregation shall stone him with stones outside the camp." Therefore the people stoned him to death. (See Numbers 15:32-36.)

Show Illustration #5b

In the Law God commanded that the land was to be farmed and cared for six years out of every seven. But the seventh year the land was to rest. Nothing was to be planted or harvested that year. (See Leviticus 25:1-7.) His people ignored this command. For 490 years they worked the land, never allowing it to rest. So God punished them by letting them be taken captive into the land of Babylon for 70 years. If the land had not been worked for one year out of every seven for 490 years, it would have rested for 70 years altogether. (*Teacher*: Divide 490 years by seven.) For exactly 70 years His people suffered as slaves to the Babylonians. (See Jeremiah 25:11.)

Show Illustration #5c

When the people of God built a movable tent of worship (the tabernacle), God Himself started a fire on the brass altar, a fire which was to be kept burning always. (See Leviticus 9:23-24; 6:12-13.) Two priests, Nadab and Abihu, instead of using the fire which God had begun, used fire which they themselves lit and offered incense at a time that God had not commanded. (See Exodus 30:7-9.) Because they had not worshiped God according to His commandment, He sent another fire and killed both men. (See Leviticus 10:1-7.)

That was the Law: good but stern. It was that very law which the Galatians supposed they had to follow if they were to earn salvation. What they did not understand was that God had given the Law only to His people, the Israelites. (See Leviticus 26:46; Romans 9:4.) Nor did they understand that He gave it for their use only until Christ died. (See Romans 10:4; 2 Corinthians 3:7-11; Galatians 3:19; 4:4-5; Hebrews 7:11-12.) Paul explained that no one can ever be declared right with God by doing good deeds and performing good ceremonies (that is, law-keeping).

Because people cannot be saved by keeping laws, they need the *only* thing that can save them: God's grace. Let's see how grace works.

2. GRACE IS GOD'S KINDNESS, LOVE AND FAVOR TO THOSE WHO DO NOT DESERVE IT

Show Illustration #6a

We'll suppose that your mother had a beautiful bowl (or some other piece of pottery). She placed great value on it and asked you not to handle it. One day you disobeyed her and picked it up.

Show Illustration #6b

It slipped from your hand, crashed to the ground, and broke into hundreds of pieces. You could not possibly put it together again. You knew that your mother would punish you. That is what you deserved.

Show Illustration #6c

When your mother saw what had happened, she got tears in her eyes. But instead of punishing you for your disobedience, she took you into her arms and said, "I forgive you." You neither earned your mother's forgiveness nor deserved it in any way. You had been disobedient and deserved her punishment, but she chose to forgive you.

This is similar to what God did in giving Christ to die for us. We call this "grace." (See Romans 3:24; Hebrews 2:9.) By His grace God forgives our sin even though we don't deserve forgiveness. (See Ephesians 1:7; 2:5, 8-9.) But He does more: He justifies us. That is, He declares righteous (in right standing with Himself) every sinner who trusts in Him. (See Acts 13:39; Romans 5:17, 21; Titus 3:7.) God saves us and justifies us because of His wonderful grace, His love, His favor, His kindness.

3. JOSEPH'S KINDNESS TO HIS BROTHERS IS AN EXAMPLE OF GRACE

Long before Paul wrote his letter to the Galatians, long before God gave His law to His people, a man named Joseph illustrated grace in a remarkable way. His grace can't compare with God's grace, but it will help us to understand the grace of God.

Joseph was one of 12 brothers. Their father's name was Jacob. Because Joseph was born when his father was old, his father loved him in a special way. This made Joseph's older brothers jealous. When Jacob made Joseph a beautiful coat, they became so angry that they hated Joseph. Then Joseph had two strange dreams. In one dream Joseph and his brothers were in the field, tying up bundles of grain. Amazingly, the brothers' bundles bowed down to Joseph's bundle. In the other dream, the sun and moon and 11 stars bowed down to Joseph. These dreams made the brothers even more angry. They cried, "Do you think that some day you will rule over us and we will bow down to you?" (See Genesis 37:1-11)

Show Illustration #7

As their hatred grew, they wished they could get rid of Joseph. One day they found a group of men who were willing to buy Joseph and take him to Egypt where he would be a slave. The brothers were delighted. They sold Joseph, thinking, *Now we are done with him forever.* (Later they lied to their father, telling him that Joseph had been killed by wild beasts.)

How do you think Joseph felt? How would you feel if your brothers hated you so much they would sell you to be a slave? Would you be angry? Would you hate your brothers?

In Egypt, Joseph became a servant in the house of Potiphar, the captain of the king's guards. He did his work so well and so willingly that Potiphar put him in charge of all the other servants. But Joseph's problems were not over. Potiphar's wife told some lies about him and Joseph was thrown into prison. Even there Joseph didn't get angry. He did not say, "This is unfair! I don't deserve to be in prison." Instead, Joseph was content to trust God wherever He allowed him to be. Because he was such a good prisoner, Joseph was placed in charge of all the other prisoners. (See Genesis 39.)

Years passed until one day the king had a disturbing dream. When none of the wise men of Egypt could tell the meaning of the dream, the king was told about Joseph. He sent for him. God gave Joseph the meaning of the king's dream. Joseph warned him, saying, "O king, for seven years there will be much food in the land. But for the seven years that follow, there will be no food. People will starve unless you begin to collect and save food during these next seven years."

The king was grateful for the warning. He said, "There is none so wise as you are. From now on, you will rule over my house. Whatever you say will be done in my kingdom. Only on my throne will I be greater than you." (See Genesis 41:1-40)

For the next seven years, Joseph took charge of storing the grain in Egypt. When the famine came, there was plenty to eat. But back in Joseph's homeland, where his brothers lived with their father, there was no food.

Show Illustration #8

The brothers came down to Egypt in search of food and bowed low before the man in charge (whom they did not recognize). Joseph's dream had come true. His own brothers were bowing low before him. Imagine how afraid they were when they learned that the ruler in Egypt was really their own brother whom they had hated and sold as a slave.

Joseph understood their fear and said, "Do not be afraid nor angry with yourselves that you sold me here. God sent me before you to save your lives . . . .You thought evil against me, but God meant it for good." (See Genesis 42:1-6; 45:1-15.)

Years later when God gave the Law, He said that if a man stole another and sold him, he should be put to death. Although Joseph's brothers had done just that, Joseph did not kill them. Instead he loved them, he fed them, he forgave them. Did they deserve his kindness? No, they did not.

Suppose that Joseph had killed his brothers. Can you imagine how sad that would have made their father? Because Joseph loved his father, he would not harm his brothers.

4. BECAUSE OF GOD'S GRACE, CHRIST DIED FOR ALL OUR SINS
Galatians 3:13

Joseph was a man of grace. But God's grace is even more wonderful. You will want to write in your notebooks: Grace is the love, kindness, favor and forgiveness which God freely gives to us who do not deserve it. He does this because Christ died for us.

Because of God's grace, the Lord Jesus died for every sinner. Because of God's grace, you have heard the Gospel. By God's grace, you will be saved if you recognize that you are a sinner and come to Christ for forgiveness. "For by grace are you saved through faith; and that not of yourselves: it is the gift of God: not of works, lest any man should boast" (Ephesians 2:8-9).

Will you accept God's love, His kindness, His favor, His forgiveness–His grace–right now?

If you are already a child of God, will you thank Him for His wonderful grace? Each time you pray during the coming week, think of God's grace and thank Him for it.

Lesson 3
A CONTRAST BETWEEN LAW AND GRACE

NOTE TO THE TEACHER

In today's lesson we shall study an event recorded in Genesis. The Apostle Paul refers to it in the fourth chapter of Galatians. The people involved–Abraham, Sarah, Hagar, Isaac, and Ishmael–were real people. Their lives and experiences were examples to the Galatians and to us even today. (See 1 Corinthians 10:6, 11.) Paul uses this particular set of circumstances to show the Galatians the false teaching into which they had fallen. He uses the story to answer for the fifth time in this Epistle, the question: Is the believer under the Law? (See Galatians 2:19-21; 3:1-3, 25, 26; 4:4-6, 9, 31.)

The two sons of Abraham–Isaac and Ishmael–didn't like each other. Their descendants, the Jews (descended from Isaac) and the Arabs (descended from Ishmael), have never been friendly since that time. They are enemies in the land of Israel today.

Scripture to be studied: Galatians 4, 5; Genesis 16; 21:1-21

The *aim* of the lesson: To show that those who insist on obeying the Law in order to be saved are slaves; those who receive God's grace are free.

What your students should *know*: To live according to the Law is slavery; to live in grace is freedom.

What your students should *feel*: A sense of relief that they do not have to earn their salvation.

What your students should *do*:
Unsaved: Put their entire trust in the Son of God who, because of God's grace, died in our place.
Saved: Thank God that because of His grace, they did not have to earn salvation.

Lesson outline (for the teacher's and students' notebooks):

1. Instead of trusting God completely, Abraham and Sarah chose to help Him keep His promise.
2. Abraham had two sons rather than only one as God intended (Galatians 4:22-23).
3. God ordered Abraham to send away the slaves, Hagar and Ishmael. His promised blessing was on Isaac (Galatians 4:30).
4. All who live under the Law are slaves. Those who accept God's grace are free (Galatians 5:1-3).

The verse to be memorized:

Christ hath redeemed us from the curse of the law, being made a curse for us. (Galatians 3:13a)

THE LESSON

Paul was puzzled. *Why,* he thought, *would the Galatian believers want to accept the false ways which they were being taught by some Jewish teachers who claimed to be Christians?* The Galatians were not Jews, nor did they understand the Jewish laws and ceremonies. The Galatians were Gentiles.

They had been idol worshipers before Paul preached the Gospel to them. When they learned of the true God, they received His Son who had given Himself as a sacrifice for their sin. The false teachers said that it was also necessary for them to obey the Jewish law; that they had to become Jews in order to become Christians. So the Galatians were trying to learn the Jewish laws and ceremonies.

Paul reminded the Galatians that there was a time when they were slaves to false gods (idols) which did not even exist. "Now that you have received the Gospel and are free men and sons of God, why are you turning back to being slaves? Would you want to go back to serving your dead idols? No? Then why do you want to be slaves to the Jewish law?" (See Galatians 4:8-9.) How foolishly the Galatians were behaving! They had been freed from one kind of slavery but were willing to be led into another.

Paul said, "Oh, I wish I were with you now, for I am fearful and worried about you. Listen! The Law cannot save you; all it can do is curse you if you break it!" Then Paul told the Galatians something which had happened many, many years before. The event is recorded in the first book of the Bible, Genesis.

Abraham was a man who loved and obeyed God. He lived 430 years before God gave the Law to the Israelites. Even though he couldn't even know the Law, he lived a life of faith in God.

Show Illustration #9

One day God gave Abraham a special promise. He said, "Look up into the sky and try to count the stars. Just as there are more stars than you can count, so some day your children and your children's children will be more than can be counted. All the nations of the earth will one day be blessed through you." (See Genesis 15:1-6.) What a wonderful promise!

Years passed. Still Abraham and his wife Sarah had no children. How could God's promise of "more children than can be counted" come true if there was not even one child in their family?

1. INSTEAD OF TRUSTING GOD COMPLETELY, ABRAHAM AND SARAH CHOSE TO HELP HIM KEEP HIS PROMISE

Surely Abraham and Sarah should have known that when God promises something, He always gives it. But they grew impatient.

Sarah got an idea which she shared with Abraham. It was something she had learned from the customs of her old home town (Ur on the Euphrates River). "Abraham," she said, "God has kept me from having a baby. But I have an Egyptian maid,

Hagar. If you take her for your wife, we might still have children." Abraham agreed with her and took Hagar, the slave girl, as his wife. (See Genesis 16:1-4.)

Sarah knew that she had done wrong. Furthermore, because Hagar was going to have a child, she refused to show respect for Sarah, her mistress. She no longer behaved like a servant. This made Sarah unhappy. No wonder!

She had planned what she would do without waiting for God's direction. So she complained to Abraham. She admitted she had done wrong.

Abraham said, "She's your maid. Do what you want with her."

Show Illustration #10

Sarah must have been harsh with Hagar, for Hagar ran away, out into the wilderness. There the angel of God came and talked with her. He told her to return to Sarah and obey her. He promised Hagar that she would have a son, Ishmael, who would one day become the father of a multitude of people. (See Genesis 16:6-15.)

2. ABRAHAM HAD TWO SONS RATHER THAN ONLY ONE AS GOD INTENDED
Galatians 4:22-23

So Hagar returned to Sarah's house. Not long after that, her son Ishmael was born.

Thirteen years passed. God again spoke to Abraham, reminding him of the promise He had made years before. Abraham thought that Ishmael was the son whom God had promised. But God said, "No, Ishmael will become the father of many people; but the son whom I promised will be borne by Sarah."

By a miracle, Sarah (who was much too old to have a child) became the mother of a baby boy, Isaac. By then, Ishmael, Hagar's son, was almost 14. He didn't treat the new baby kindly. He was jealous of this other son of Abraham, because now his father's wealth would be divided between him and Isaac.

One day when Sarah saw Ishmael mocking young Isaac, she became angry. She said to Abraham, "Throw out this slave woman and her son. This son of a slave will not be an heir with my son Isaac!" (See Genesis 21:8-10.)

Both Ishmael and Isaac were Abraham's sons. Even though one was born to a slave woman, Abraham loved them both. How could he send Ishmael away?

3. GOD ORDERED ABRAHAM TO SEND AWAY HAGAR AND ISHMAEL
Galatians 4:30

Show Illustration #11

While Abraham was grieving, God spoke to him, saying, "Don't be downhearted. Send Ishmael and his mother away, as Sarah has said. The promise I made to you will come through Isaac. But I shall make a large nation from Ishmael because he, too, is your son." God kept that promise by making Ishmael the father of all the Arab nations.

When God said the promise would come through Isaac, He was speaking of Jesus, the Promised One, the Saviour of the world, the One who would be born through Isaac's family. (See Romans 9:7.) The Saviour would not come through Hagar, a slave, but through Sarah, a free woman.

The Apostle Paul reminded the Galatians that Abraham had two sons, one by the slave woman and the other by the free woman. He said, "The child of the slave woman (Ishmael) had an ordinary birth. But the other son (Isaac) was a miracle child, born as God promised."

4. ALL WHO LIVE UNDER THE LAW ARE SLAVES. THOSE WHO ACCEPT GOD'S GRACE ARE FREE
Galatians 5:1-3

Show Illustration #12a

Paul explained that this event has this hidden meaning: Hagar, the slave, is like the Law. Because she was a slave, her child was a slave. Those who live according to the works of the Law are like slaves.

Show Illustration #12b

But Sarah, the free woman, is like grace. Her son, Isaac, was free. He inherited all that his father Abraham owned.

Show Illustration #12c

We who believe in Jesus, having received God's gift of salvation through faith, are also free. We aren't slaves to the Law. We are the free children of God. Those who are slaves to the Law will never have eternal life. They will be cast out just as Hagar was. Those who have accepted the gift of salvation through God's wonderful grace receive the inheritance of eternal life.

Are you a slave who is trying to earn your salvation? If so, will you turn instead to the Saviour? Place all your trust in Him. Remember it is because of God's grace that Christ died for you. If you are already a child of God, thank Him that because Christ died in your place, you never had to do a thing to earn eternal life. "Christ hath redeemed us from the curse of the Law, being made a curse for us: for it is written, Cursed is every one that hangeth on a tree" (Galatians 3:13).

> **NOTE TO THE TEACHER**
> Your students should make notes on the illustration that Paul used in Galatians 4:21-31:
>
> Abraham, the father = the father of the Arab and Hebrew nations.
> Sarah, the free woman = grace.
> Hagar, the slave = law.
> Isaac, the son of the free woman = those who, by grace, inherit eternal life by being born into the family of God through faith in Christ Jesus.
> Ishmael, the son of the slave = those who cannot inherit eternal life because they are slaves to the Law, trusting in their works to earn God's gift of salvation.

Lesson 4
LAW AND GRACE REVIEWED

NOTE TO THE TEACHER

In the previous three lessons we have examined law and grace, contrasting them with each other. Now we shall review these terms.

It would be helpful to read Romans 10 and 11 for more information on the subject of law and grace. Paul discussed Israel in those chapters. The Israelites refused the Gospel of grace, choosing rather to do the works of the Law. Because of this refusal, God has set Israel aside for a time and is freely offering His salvation to the people of the Gentile nations (as well as to any individual Jews who receive Christ).

The situation remains the same today as in Paul's day. There are some people of the Hebrew nation who have listened to the truth and have, by God's grace, received the gift of salvation by faith in Christ. But there are many more who cling to the ceremonies of the Law, refusing to believe in Jesus as their Messiah and Saviour. The same is true among the Gentiles and may be true of some whom you teach. Many will receive the Gospel of grace. Others will hold to the tradition of good works. Present this lesson prayerfully and carefully so that your students may understand the simplicity of God's plan of salvation.

Scripture to be studied: Galatians 3 and 4; Exodus 20:18-21; Hebrews 12:18-21

The *aim* of the lesson: To show that the Law is a fearful thing which keeps us away from God because we are sinners. Only by God's grace can we come to Him through Christ Jesus.

>**What your students should *know*:** The Law kept people away from God; grace brings people to God.
>
>**What your students should *feel*:** Joy because they do not have to depend on their own good works to save them.
>
>**What your students should *do*:**
>
>>*Unsaved:* Give themselves wholly to Christ, depending on His grace.
>>
>>*Saved:* Ask their Father God to tell them something they can do to show their love for Him.

Lesson outline (for the teacher's and students' notebooks):

1. If we break one part of the Law, we have broken all of it.
2. Because of God's grace, we who trust in Christ are not slaves but sons.
3. The Law keeps people away from God.
4. God's grace brings people to Himself through Christ.

The verse to be memorized:

Christ hath redeemed us from the curse of the law, being made a curse for us. (Galatians 3:13a)

THE LESSON

Listen while I read something written by the Apostle Paul to the believers in Rome. He mentioned that some Israelites received God's gift of salvation by faith. Then he says, "And if they are saved from the penalty of sin because of God's grace, then they have done nothing to earn it. If they had earned it, then God's grace would not be a free gift." (See Romans 11:6.)

We have been talking about law and grace in these lessons. Who can remind us again of the meaning of the term "grace"? (The love, kindness, favor, and forgiveness shown to us by God because of Christ's death. Grace is completely undeserved or unearned. *Teacher*: You may want to allow some time to review the lesson on Joseph.)

What do we mean by the term "law"? (The rules and ceremonies which God gave to the Jews. These rules were strict and carried severe punishments for disobedience.)

Law and grace are really opposite. (Review the Ishmael and Isaac lesson.) Those who live by the Law are like slaves, fearful of making a mistake, always receiving punishment for failure. Those who live by grace are free, knowing that Christ has already taken their punishment.

In the verse which we read from Romans, Paul says that grace and law cannot be mixed. Because we are saved by grace, works are not needed. Nor will God accept the person who tries to earn salvation. If we had to work in order to he saved, then salvation would not be a gift from God. Works are not included in our salvation. We do not buy or earn our way into God's family. We must be *born* into His family.

No one ever becomes the king or queen of England unless he or she is born into the royal family. A person might spend years working and trying to become England's king or queen. That would do no good. The only way to get that position, is by being born into it. So it is with salvation. You cannot work for it in any way. You must be born into God's family by placing your faith in the Lord Jesus.

Our memory verse tells us that we are cursed by the Law. That is, because we are sinners, we deserve punishment.

1. IF WE BREAK ONE PART OF THE LAW, WE HAVE BROKEN ALL OF IT

We can't possibly keep every part of the Law perfectly. Yet if we fail in only one part, we are guilty of breaking the whole law. "For if a person obeys all the laws except one, he is guilty of breaking them all" because he has sinned against God who gave all the Law. (See James 2:10.)

Maybe we can make this a little clearer by doing a bit of pretending. Suppose you are walking along a path at the edge of a steep cliff. Even though you are being very careful you trip and drop over the edge of the cliff. Down . . . down . . . down you fall!

Show Illustration #13

If there happened to be a chain securely fastened to a rock and you were able to catch hold of it, you would be safe. But wait! That chain is made of many links. How many links would have to break before you would fall? Only one broken link would ruin the chain.

The Law is like that chain. You can try hard to obey the Law. But if you break even one small part, you are guilty of breaking the whole law. You then deserve punishment for having broken the Law.

Our memory verse says that you are cursed by the Law. You are condemned. You are guilty. But our memory verse also says that Christ has already taken the punishment which the Law demands. He took the death curse of your sin on Himself. He was put to death because of your sins. He was raised again to declare you in right standing with God. (See Romans 4:25.)

2. BECAUSE OF GOD'S GRACE, WE WHO TRUST IN CHRIST ARE NOT SLAVES BUT SONS

Christ came to free you from the slavery of the Law.

Those who receive Christ as Saviour have been born into God's family. Instead of being treated as servants (slaves) they are placed in the high position of sons. (See Galatians 4:6-7.)

Show Illustration #14

The Greeks and Romans practiced an interesting custom. When a boy was born into a family, he was called a child until he reached a certain age. As a child, he was treated much like a servant. When he was old enough to be considered an adult, he went through a son-placing ceremony. His father dressed him in a toga, a garment worn by a man. After this, he was no longer called a child, but a son. From then on he was regarded as a partner with his father. He was then the heir of all his father owned. He had reached the position of sonship, which was much higher than childhood.

Christ made it possible for us to have the position of sonship with God. God sees the one who has been born into His family as though he wears a robe of righteousness. (See Isaiah 61:10; Revelation 19:8.) He sees him the same way in which He sees His Son, Jesus. (See 1 Corinthians 3:23.) If you are a son of God, you can call Him "Father." (See Galatians 4:6.)

When you were only a baby, one of the first words you learned to say was Papa (or Dada), meaning Father. When you would see your father coming toward you, you would call out to him. He was special to you. You loved him in a personal way, because you knew him better than any other man. Paul reminds you that the Holy Spirit living within you makes it possible for you to know God in such a personal, loving way that you can call Him Father. (In the English language, the word *Abba* in Galatians 4:6 could be translated *Daddy, or My own very dear Father*.) When Paul wrote his letter to the Galatian believers he could hardly believe they would choose to live a life of fear under the Law rather than enjoy the freedom of God's grace. Why would anyone choose to be a slave, he thought, when they could instead be free and have all the privileges given to a son of God?

3. THE LAW KEEPS PEOPLE AWAY FROM GOD

Did the Galatians understand the fear that was connected with the giving of the Law that meant slavery? Did they know how afraid of God the Israelites were when the Law was given? (See Exodus 20:19-20.) Let us see what it was like then.

Show Illustration #15

God commanded that the people were to be kept away from the Sinai mountain, away from God's holy presence. They were not even to touch the border of the mountain. If either a person or a beast did touch it, it would mean instant death. (See Exodus 19:12-13.)

Moses was terrified when he climbed Mount Sinai. The mountain shook with a mighty earthquake. The top of the mountain was covered with smoke. There was flashing lightning and crashing thunder. The Lord came down to the mountain in fire. There, with the people kept away from Him, He gave the Law. (See Exodus 20:18-21; Hebrews 12:18-21.)

The Law was given to Moses in a frightening way, and it continued to bring fear to the people. Disobedience to any part of the Law meant death. The Law was severe indeed.

Show Illustration #16

Those who lived under law did not dare approach God directly in order to have their sins covered. Each one brought an animal sacrifice to the priest who went to God for the sinner. The Law kept sinners away from God.

4. GOD'S GRACE BRINGS PEOPLE TO HIMSELF THROUGH CHRIST

It is entirely different for those who live under grace. Jesus Christ's sacrifice for sin makes it possible for believers to approach God directly. (See Ephesians 2:13; Hebrews 10:19-22.) If you have received Christ as Saviour, God sees you clothed in His righteousness, bought by Jesus' blood. (See 2 Corinthians 5:21.) You no longer need to fear God's anger and punishment. The Lord Jesus has already received the punishment which you deserve for your sins. You are accepted in Him. (See Ephesians 1:6.)

It is glorious to live under grace. Instead of being held off from God by fear, you can come to Him through His Son, Jesus Christ. Because He poured out His life blood on Calvary, you have mercy instead of judgment. You have pardon instead of punishment. (See Hebrews 12:22-24.)

Have you confessed to God that you are a sinner? Have you told Him that you believe that the Lord Jesus is His Son? Have you received the free gift of God's grace by placing your trust in the Lord Jesus Christ? Or are you still under the slavery of the Law–trying to please God by doing good works?

If you have already received the Lord Jesus, thank God that you can call Him Father. Tell Him right now how much you love Him. Ask Him to show you what you can do for Him today to prove you love Him.